MISSING, ABORTED, HALF-ALIVE

Progress and Development

or

Persons and Freedom

I0171043

by:

Vernon Molloy

Table of Contents

Foreword..3
Mission Statement..4
Specific Proposals..5
Internal Gestation..6
Genetic and Cultural Recapitulations..............18
External Gestation: Wombs with a View.........27
Progress or Persons...40
Ayes Everywhere...45
Self-Determination..51
How Conversations Happen.............................52
A Solution...67
On-Demand Economies....................................70
Resources:...80

Foreword

In 1919, the First World War just ended, William
Butler Yeats' described a tumultuous world in
The Second Coming:

> *Mere anarchy is loosed upon the world,*
> *The blood-dimmed tide is loosed, and everywhere*
> *... Things fall apart; the centre cannot hold; `*
> *The ceremony of innocence is drowned;*
> *The best lack all conviction, while the worst*
> *Are full of passionate intensity.*

A century later, North Korea and the United
States are brandishing nuclear weapons and
nuclear non-proliferation treaties are being
rescinded or close to expiring.

Mutually Assured Destruction (MAD) no longer
seems an adequate deterrent.

This book describes bottom-up rather than top-
down ways to think about such difficulties.[1]

---

1   These suggestions are from ruminations already written
    down or still distilling themselves: see *Resources*.

Progress and Development

Mission Statement

The world is complex and becoming more so. The sum total of knowledge is doubling year over year.

As this happens, every person's sense of possibility and responsibility shrinks. We turn away from one another. We retreat into virtual worlds. We collapse into tribal loyalties.

This was first noticed by Buckminster Fuller, who provided a way to take its measure:

> ... human knowledge is doubling every 13 months. According to IBM, the build out of the "internet of things" will lead to the doubling of knowledge every 12 hours.[2]

A way to respond is to challenge the granular certainties parsing experiences into the bits that make complexity possible. The sense we have that we are things, that reality is similarly constituted, sanctions dividing what is going on into ever-smaller events and a blizzard of causal relationships linking them together.

We watch in amazement as this Rube Goldberg contraption lurches from moment to moment.

This is where I hope to be of service. I hope to demonstrate the dubious nature of beliefs underpinning these proceedings. My suggestions will not replace old

_____

2   https://www.glennbeck.com/2014/04/07/will-human-knowledge-soon-have-the-power-to-double-every-12-hours/

understandings with new certainties. My ambition is to revive the curiosity and skepticism we all enjoyed when we were children.

This is fun, and worth doing for political and economic reasons. Human beings need chain-letter explosions of skepticism and mischief. We need to become as difficult to herd as free-range chickens.

With an exception described at the end of this book, we need to stop forming into platoons.

Specific Proposals

- Reduce human beings' chronological age by defining birthdays as the onset of puberty.

- Separate gestation into two intervals: time in wombs and time in the world before puberty.

- Demote consciousness from its role as the seat of moral and rational agency and free will.

- Conscious episodes facilitate cognitive proceedings. Like blackboards, they do not author, collate or evaluate symbols written upon them.

- Not all human beings become persons, although most have the capacity to do so. Getting this ratio close to 1 : 1 is not merely a Golden Rule, it is the only survivable option.

Internal Gestation

As societies become congested and complex, ordinary experiences become focused and minute. Individuals struggle under economic pressures and a blizzard of information.

This discourages macroeconomic (Big Picture) thinking. Yet the need to pay attention has never been greater. Human beings no longer live in a state of nature wherein what is going on around us can be trusted.

What happens when thousands or millions of business plans are beavering away in ways Mother Nature did not anticipate?

Although the consequences bear upon ordinary lives, human and otherwise, such worries are left to politicians with partisan agendas and academics whose observations have little traction in ordinary affairs. No one is attempting to figure out what happens when minute decisions and problems clump together and have consequences of their own. We have a vague sense that these unbidden consequences are accumulating, but we also understand that no one is responsibility, or that no one can do anything beyond wishing official responses Godspeed.

When populations were small and spread out, paying attention to local issues and nothing but made sense. Those days are gone. We are overrunning the world and conspiring against one another and our future selves.

I am going to discuss two examples. They are interesting in themselves and serve as proxies for other issues. The first is the way contraceptives are only discussed in terms of unwanted pregnancies and sexually transmitted diseases, with little interest in the political and economic consequences of managed fertility.

The second is the way conversations about abortion—in some sense, a form of belated contraception—focuses narrowly upon women's vs. embryos' rights.

These conversations are focused locally or micro-economically. They are important in their own right, and they must occur before macroeconomic discussions become possible. However, no matter how widespread, local conversations do not substitute for Big Picture discussions.

For example, local discussions of contraceptives and abortion fail to:

1. Consider the emergent nature of life. Conception, birth, death ... can be thought of as episodes along narratives that began before conceptions and never really end. Albert Einstein's and Adolf Hitler's lives continue to enlarge possibilities on one hand and diminish them on the other.

2. Pay attention to the notion of *prevented* lives.

3. Recognize that not all human beings become persons, and that such failures are significant.

Progress and Development

To clarify 2 & 3, I propose to expand the meaning of *abortion* to include external (non-uterine) events that: (1) prevent conceptions from occurring, or (2) prevent conceived beings from becoming persons.

On this reckoning, aborting events are no longer restricted to surgical interventions in wombs. They can include prenatal and postnatal factors: contraceptives, the age and health of parents, environmental toxins, day care costs and much else.

Since abortions can occur outside of wombs, they can be

> Abortions can be partial or complete

thought of as *partial* or *complete*. Complete abortions include murders, fatal accidents and unnatural death by any means, including military activities. Partial abortions—a new notion—leaves human beings half-alive, but crippled since they have been prevented from becoming persons.

Ironically, many of the proceedings this enlarged definition includes flow from progress and development achievements. As Illustration 1 demonstrates, during the last half of the 20th century, millions of lives have been failing to turn up in nations scoring well on the *Human Development Index*.

This is important for another reason. Any population whose fertility rate falls below 2.1 (2.3 in developing nations) is engaging in a kind of self-administered, voluntary genocide. This consequence of prosperity has never been seen in other species.

Lives that would have occurred in 'normal circumstances' should be included in abortion discussions. Pro-lifers do some of this work, but seem to have little interest in preemptive or post-parturition abortions.

The Catholic Church prohibits contraceptives and does a good deal of hand-wringing about masturbation— conceptions are not occurring because sperm is being wasted. This is an excellent example of micro-economic thinking. If one believes that the concern is legitimate, then it is surely relevant that the Catholic Church has been silent in the face evidence that sperm counts have been falling in western nations, more than 60 per cent in 40 years.

This decline is usually attributed to hormonal and chemical by-products of commercial activities, a consequence micro-economic moralities easily overlook.

ᎣᏇᎢᏇᎣᏇᎢᏇᎣᏇᎢᏇ

From this vantage point, abortions can be thought of as occurring outside of wombs. As Illustrations 1 & 2 demonstrate, high fertility rates have been occurring in the context of slowly increasing populations. Lots of people were being born but, until recently, most did not survive to become parents.

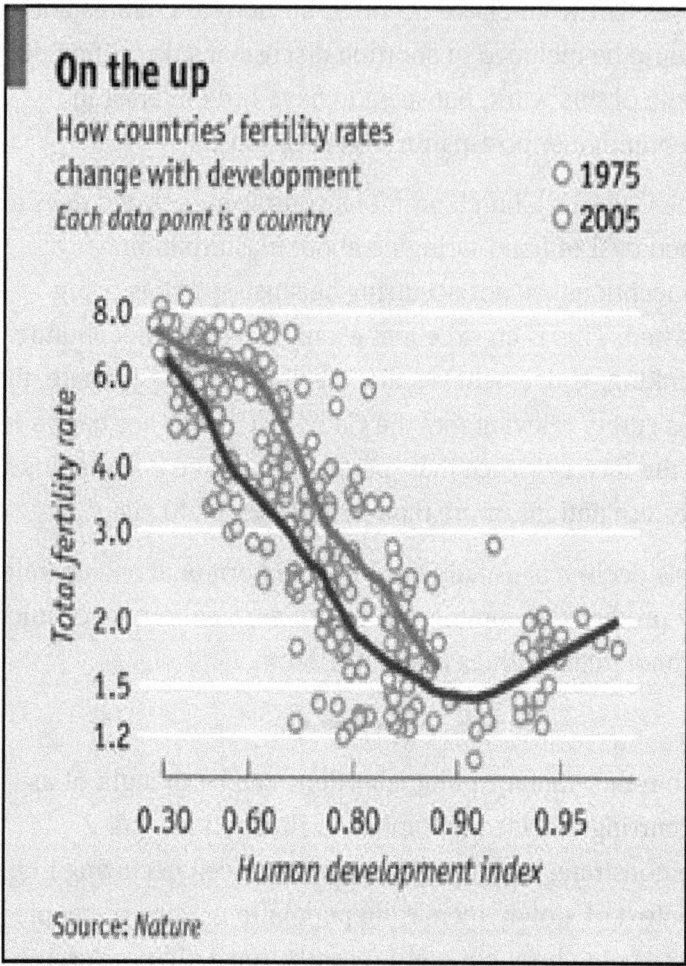

Illustration 1: Fertility and Prosperity

World population (1700-2000) and population projections (2000-2100)

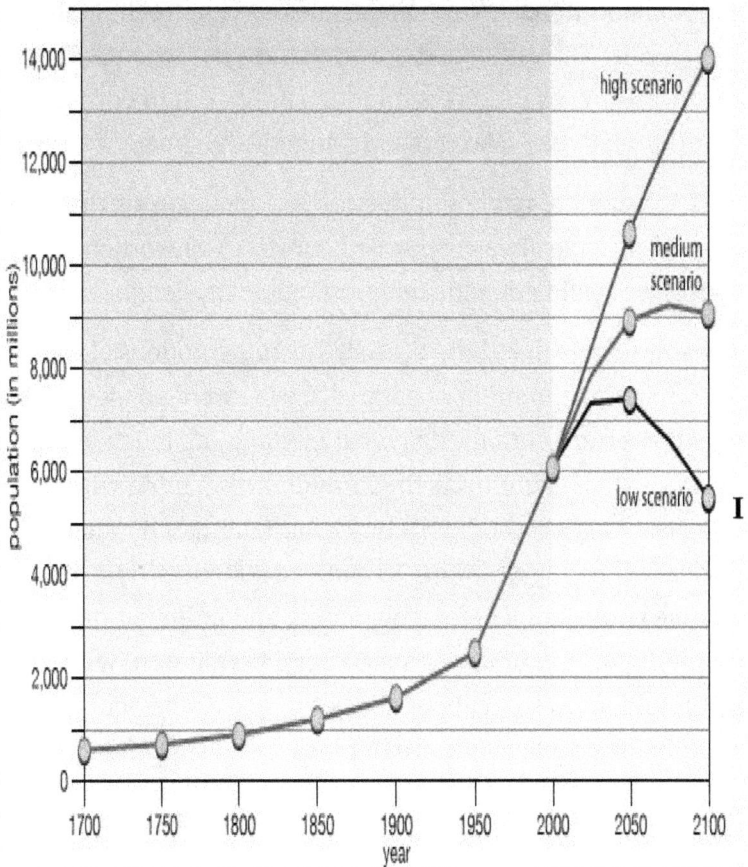

Source: United Nations Department of Economic and Social Affairs/Population Division 2004   © 2012 Encyclopædia Britannica, Inc.

llustration 2: Population Growth Rates

Progress and Development

The events generating these statistics can be thought of as external abortions. We are not accustomed to thinking in such terms. Starvation and epidemics are not regarded as acts of nature. Wars and revolutions are traced to corrupt or glorious leaders—who rarely decline the honour!

This 'great man' reading of historical events means that most of us have always regarded ourselves as workers, consumers, soldiers, innocent bystanders or victims.

The problem is that these are self-fulfilling notions. They lead to moral and rational paralysis. We rarely ponder whether we are complicit in what is going on, much less in terms of what is not occurring. Failures to grapple with climate change and military threats are discussed in terms of leaders achieving or failing to achieve solutions. The idea that we could simply stop consuming and polluting or murdering one another without asking permission, without being told to do so, without checking to see whether coordinating agreements are in place ... never occurs to us.

Perhaps we do not want to do sensible stuff and look overeager or foolish.

The closest we come to notions of distributed responsibility is to recognize that individuals sometimes inadvertently enable others to do harm. There is no accountability however. *Unwitting enabling* is not indictable.

ᠣᠭᡃ᠌ᢆᠣᡃᠭ᠌ᢆᠣᡃᠭᢆ

These micro calculations also mean corporations and nations get a pass. Corporate activities and agendas occur in the absence of indictable *mens rea* episodes in employees, customers and even boards of directors. Nations similarly exonerated. Soldiers doing their duty under chains of command are innocent by definition. Military commanders receive their marching orders from governments. Governments are bound to electors whose responsibilities are restricted to casting or destroying ballots—or, if one really wants to make a statement, refusing to participate.

The result is that "Who is really in charge?" questions rarely detain us. People see themselves as bystanders or victims of greedy or malignant leaders or corporations. Duly-elected or properly promoted individuals acknowledge responsibilities in shallow ways. Responsibilities are defined, measured and *conferred* by processes and institutions. Leaders and the wealthy sleep soundly because they believe that they are acting out the deep preferences of populations, even if this involves functioning as cannon fodder or commercial assets.

What is the alternative? Billions of human beings much be orchestrated into coherent, socialized behaviours. We have settled upon democratic capitalism is the best strategy to achieve the most gain for the least pain. In proper democracies, defective leaders can be replaced in orderly fashion. Concerned voters stay their hand for another reason. A next election could very well return the same or worse politicians or agendas! The social contract citizens undertake

Progress and Development

is to wait for and respect the outcome of democratic elections.

In other words, democracies allow citizens to kick problems down the road in circumspect ways. Politicians and corporate leaders love democracies for reasons of their own. They harvest profits and garner power effortlessly. They can deny malignant agendas in that fully-fledged *mens rea* conscious episodes are rarely required. The economic and political mechanisms generating their lovely lives have been baked into business as usual and require only occasional tinkering. The result is that most politicians and corporate leaders could pass lie detector tests with flying colours. Mr. Hitler, Mr. Trump, Kim Jung-un ... could successfully deny accusations that they are consciously up to no good.

Such proceedings were described by Mr. Yeats—dreadful events, with no one responsible. Mankind's moral crisis is that moral crises have become impossible.

 መግ መግ መግ

A possible response involves enlarging the meaning of gestation and demoting person-hood from the status of innate endowment or Divine incarnation. On this account, gestation includes experiences until puberty shuts down general curiosity and focused, fully-fledged adults emerge to make their reproductive run, as all creatures must.

In adults, information will now be curated, assessed, assimilated and responded to according to congruence with information, values and priorities absorbed during external gestation. This is when it makes sense to say that birthing has occurred. Genotypes have become fully-fledged phenotypes and cultural tanks have been topped up.

The results will now be tested for fitness: Do these individuals, *and the circumstances and experiences that constituted external gestation,* have what it takes to survive and reproduce?

Reproducing is not the only test that matters. Reproducing is a micro-economic question. The macro-economic, over-arching issue is what proportion of human beings become persons? The goal should be to make this proportion one hundred per cent or 1:1. This is doubtlessly impossible for reasons which become intuitive if we ask what proportion of hunters and gatherers achieved person-hood cultural and technological resources became part of ordinary experience.

As well, many cultural practices and technological embellishments are now getting in the way of human beings achieving person-hood.

In particular, enlarging the way gestation is understood would improve this proportion:

1. Instinctive concern for the unborn would be extended. This would diminish tendencies to over-nurture and over-protect children because they are regarded as innate persons. What counts as

15

wholesome would be informed by the now clear need for progressively demanding experiences.

The move from womb to world is the biggest shock human beings experience. The instinctive response —to create a secure external womb—is the reason human beings survived life on the ground for thousands of years. The problem is that this instinct is now being amplified with powerful technologies and cultural resources. The result is that, whenever resources permit, external wombs come perilously close to replicating internal wombs.

2.   This is where progress and development intersect with nascent human beings and cause half-aborted lives.

3.   An elongated understanding of gestation will resist vacuous renderings of uterine life: endless ease, no demands, smart phones in strollers, 8 hours of daily screen time.

4.   Men would be less able to deny responsibility and involvement in the way children turn into adults. Historically, militarily, economically ... men have done far more aborting than women. This has gone unnoticed because men use other terms to talk about

what they get up to: patriotism, bread-winning, job jars, hen-pecked lives ....[3]

5. Enlarging the gestation interval until puberty expands Richard Dawkins' notion of extended phenotypes in interesting ways. The circumstances involved in external gestation are included in reproductive fitness tests the way beavers, beaver dams and water security issues are evaluated in Dawkins' example.

---

3 https://www.britannica.com/science/population-biology-and-anthropology

Genetic and Cultural Recapitulations

Abortions are usually thought of as having positive consequences for the adults convening them—although not for 'candidate persons' aborted! Redefining the meaning of gestation, birthing, abortion ... allows broader consequences to be thought about.

This could be important. Human beings are no longer adapting to the world, we are changing it to correspond to our prerogatives and the agendas of corporations and nations.[4]

In every other case, evolution fine-tunes phenotypes by dividing species into male and female, shuffling DNA packages and sorting the results into winners and losers. These genotypes and phenotypes track ecological niches in straightforward ways. Because human beings have been exploring have been the adaptive benefits of big brains and prolonged dependencies, new factors—including the wholesomeness of cultural proceedings—have been added to the process.

Indeed, the activities and cumulative footprints of corporations and nations have become a factor determining

---

4   Aug 29, 2016 – Humanity's impact on the Earth is now so profound that a new geological epoch – the *Anthropocene* – needs to be declared, according to an official expert group who presented the recommendation to the International Geological Congress in Cape Town on Monday.

whether individuals survive and reproduce (Illustration 1). As a result, during the 20th century, fertility rates in nations scoring high on the Human Development Index dropped below replacement levels. The cultural and technological achievements involved reflect thousands of generations of living and dying and incremental cultural achievements.

As well, human beings' genetic legacy tracks back to the beginning of life. Until recently, biologists, (beginning with Ernst Haeckel,1834-1919) described this relationship with a formidable expression: *embryology recapitulates ontogeny* —fetuses go through recapitulations (condensed versions) of their species' evolutionary histories. Haeckel sketched what this looks like in the human instance.

Haeckel's depictions have been brought up to date but the core idea remains:

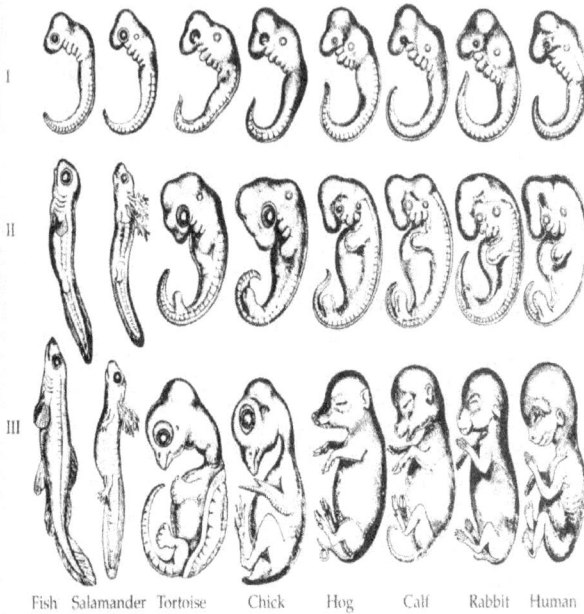

Fish Salamander Tortoise Chick Hog Calf Rabbit Human

Species' Organic Recapitulation

"Embryos do reflect the course of evolution, but that course is far more intricate and quirky than Haeckel claimed. Different parts of the same embryo can even evolve in different directions. As a result, the Bio-genetic Law was abandoned, (freeing) scientists to appreciate the full range of embryonic changes that evolution can produce ....[5]

ᎤᎤᎤ

Haeckel's recapitulation underscores the complexity of the aborting, culling, selecting ... events along evolutionary

---

5   https://en.wikipedia.org/wiki/Recapitulation_theory

trails. This is not to suggest that human beings represent an evolutionary pinnacle, but that the present generation of human beings a moral obligation to the events and lives that made us possible.

There is no way to say how this obligation should be met. However, keeping the natural world as wholesome, even-handed and variegated as possible feels right.

Across thousands of generations, our ancestors spawned languages and technologies beginning with fire, spears and stone tools. These achievements helped them eke out an existence, discuss successes and failures and figure out ways to record conversations and insights.

> Cultural riches and technological prowess have placed mankind at a crossroads.

These activities have been fine-tuning genetic and cultural legacies. We have an obligation to preserve and pass these legacies along, and improve them if possible.

The facile agendas of corporations, nations and the emergence of artificial intelligence devices should therefore be viewed skeptically. We should do everything possible to ensure that the world emerging on our watch remains wholesome and habitable. This obligation includes other species and future generations. Although it is possible to be optimistic about the way things are going (see Steven

Progress and Development

Pinker)[6], many are alarmed. Along with environmental issues and nuclear war threats, our instincts, cultural achievements and technological prowess have been spawning a new kind of existential threat:

- An elongated gestation means individuals in culturally-rich circumstances have unprecedented opportunities to to become persons. We are living longer and we have fewer torments keeping us awake at night. Diseases, fleas, lice, bedbugs and rats leave most of us along most of the time. Mosquitoes, black flies and Deer ticks lurk beyond city boundaries but fewer and fewer of us are coming across them.

- These comforts have a dark side of course. Twelve years of exposure/gestation (the words are interchangeable!) means urban stratagems have time to insinuate themselves into our lives in ways that can seem natural and wholesome. Thus, commercial and political agendas have been feasting upon human beings' mating/reproducing instincts and using the profits to finance further encroachments.

- The results include womb-cities completely aborting future generations and partially-aborting the present.

---

6   https://www.ted.com/talks/
steven_pinker_on_the_myth_of_violence

This is not the end of mischief. With eggs and children in urban baskets, police forces and armies become increasingly necessary and expensive.[7] In 2018 figures, $2.1 trillion means roughly $300 in military expenditures per capita. Since most human beings are poor, the per capita cost in wealthy nations is higher.

The capital and servicing costs of urbanized ways of living is also a significant burden. In 2018, global public debt exceeded $63 trillion: roughly, $9000 per capita, again with the lion's share in. These debts are owed by managed to manager populations. Of course, we get to live in often sophisticated circumstances. Even so, we are like cattle who have been persuaded to borrow against future milk production to finance barns and harvesting equipment. The fact that we crowing instead of bawling about our circumstances measures our confusion.

---

7   http://www.globalissues.org/article/75/world-military-spending

Progress and Development

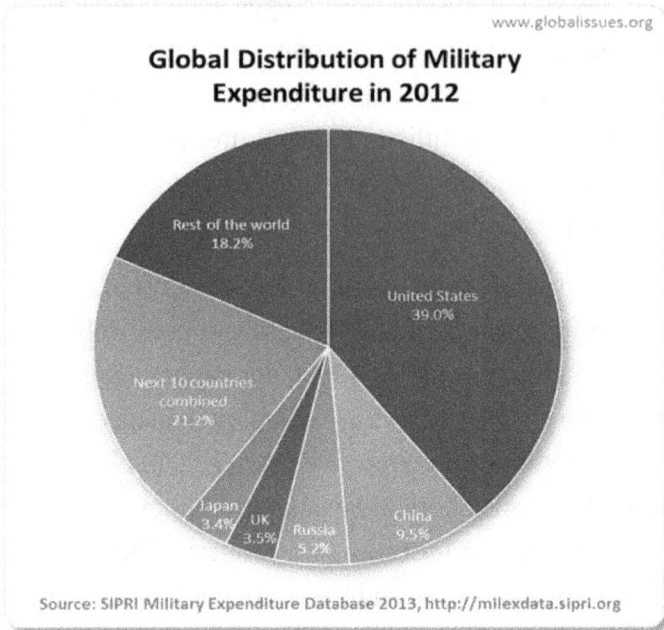

Global Distribution of Military Expenditure in 2012

Rest of the world 18.2%

United States 39.0%

Next 10 countries combined 21.2%

Japan 3.4%

UK 3.5%

Russia 5.2%

China 9.5%

Source: SIPRI Military Expenditure Database 2013, http://milexdata.sipri.org

www.globalissues.org

Military Spending as a percentage of $1.7 Trillion

ማኑ.ማኑ.ማኑ

These are serious matters. Murdering human beings is a moral issue—whether within nine months or twelve years, or any time before natural deaths occur. What we have not thought much about is that the activities referred to as progress and development may be preventing human beings from becoming persons while leaving them nominally alive.

These partial abortions could be thought of as overarching, macro-moral harms:

- Partial abortions leave human beings alive to suffer.

- Partially-aborted human beings are easily assembled into corporations, nations, religions and other enterprises.

- When individuals fail to become persons, they are likely to lead angry, dismayed and frightened lives. They seek out belligerent compensations. They participate vicariously in wealthy and powerful lives, whose achievements usually depend upon fans, workers, consumers and soldiers.

History books are filled with the results, and the world is full of individuals like those in Illustration 4. The question to ask is whether these individuals are morally-culpable or victims of person-aborting events?

Progress and Development

Kim Jong-un's Sermon on the Mount

External Gestation: Wombs with a View

Regarding gestation as the sum of events before puberty—
and puberty as the event deserving the birthday honorific—
could dissolve the paralysis herding human beings along
development road.

Why would this be so? Separating gestation into inside and
outside intervals re-frames the nature/nurture debate.
Historically, nature and nurture have been thought of as
operating sequentially and the issue has been how they
should be apportioned. The usual answer is 80% nature,
20% nurture, largely based on
research involving identical
twins separated at birth.
Dividing gestation into intra-
uterine and extra-uterine stages
does not deny the importance of
womb-based gestation, but
emphasizes the equal importance of external gestation
events. Any link in a chain is equally important because any
failure has the same consequence.

> Solving the
> nature/nurture debate by
> demonstrating that they
> have linked but
> separate domains.

There is another reason to expand the meaning of gestation.

The nature/nurture, 80%/20%, ratio has a scientific ring
since it totals to 100% which presumably means there is no
wiggly room left over. Yet this ratio is proposed by
individuals who nonetheless regard themselves as moral and
rational agents thinking, understanding and acting in ways

transcending causality or determinism. They see themselves as supernatural, as able to act ex nihilo, and as only interested in apportioning the factors responsible for their prowess.

The question is: "What prowess?" With nature + nurture summing to 100%, there is no need to talk about persons acting

> The difficulty involves segregating partially-aborted human beings from look-alike Persons.

autonomously in supernatural ways, performing analyses or having conversations more interesting than the conversations artificial intelligence devices are already capable of. Unless something is added to the mix, there is no non-anthropomorphic reason to talk about persons in grandiose terms. We think fondly of pets and regularly anthropomorphize (ascribe human characteristics to) them. I propose that we anthropomorphize human beings the same way, ascribing universal person-hood on the basis of mythologized, culturally transmitted exploits of exceptional individuals generated by fortuitous genetic and cultural endowments.

The good news is that separating gestation into intra-uterine and extra-uterine stages—and debunking the myth of person-hood as a birthright—means that the idea of *persons* can be rehabilitated from vacuous conceit to excellent ambition.

ማ፟ማ፟ማ፟

We are all born human beings. No one is born a person. Person-hood results from fortuitous combinations of nature and gestation. A useful analogy is the process of starting a fire. Successful fires require kindling, paper, matches and firewood, all carefully arranged. Once started, fires can become self-sustaining—if enough heat is generated during the kindling or gestation phase to cause an updraft and the fire starts finding fresh fuel on its own recognizance.

House fires and forest fires manage this splendidly. Oftentimes, nothing can be done except let them burn themselves out of combustibles.

This analogy creates enough wiggle room to be able to talk intelligibly about persons. Mother Nature or evolution endows individuals with whatever DNA starts them along their paths. Mother Nurture is whatever happens as individuals pass through wombs or peck their way out of eggs. Nurturing includes whatever happens as individuals become adults.

In non-human species, this interval is so short that it makes sense to speak of gestation in terms of time spent in wombs or eggs. Birthdays and first appearances are so close in time it is not worth quibbling about.

In human beings, development continues for at least a decade. Hence, the need for a different understanding of gestation and for a word differentiating post-puberty

Progress and Development

individuals into re-productively competent human beings and fully-fledged persons.

In other words, rehabilitating the meaning of persons involves denying the anthropomorphizing claim that human beings automatically become persons.

Now we are getting somewhere! Human beings can be either fully or partially aborted. The fully-aborted include anyone unnaturally terminated. The partially-aborted are individuals who survive, and may live a full life-span, but do not become persons.

Once the shock of contemplating this landscape subsides—a survey that includes most but not all history—a secular issue comes knocking. The challenge is to sort the partially-aborted from their look-alike cousins.

In Illustration 4, leaders and followers are exploiting one another's lack of person-hood. There are no winners in such proceedings.

ση.ση.ση.

Religious practices and cultural activities provide clues. Baptisms, Communions, Confirmations, Bar Mitzvahs and Bat Mitzvahs, cultural rites of passage ... define stages on the road to person-hood.

What these practices implicitly acknowledge—this is never talked about!—is that human beings regularly fail to become persons. Thus, there is a tension between what is universally believed—that human beings are persons by way of Divine Incarnation or Evolutionary Birthright—and the way cultures nurture person-hood as if individuals need all the help they can get. The reason for this inconsistency—and why it is never talked about—is that cultural and religious practices, meritocracies, inequities ... require automatically-occurring person-hood if they are to be intelligible and defensible.

If persons are understood as the fruit of DNA and gestation, responsibility for public harms and moral shortfalls would reflect social and economic deficits. These deficits could not be explained away as the direct and cumulative consequences of ex nihilo moral and rational decisions.

Indeed, in micro-moral understandings and conversations, God becomes the ultimate scapegoat and unwitting enabler of malignant circumstances.

In the alternative sketched here, responsibility gets distributed according to a simple logic. Because individuals cannot be responsible the way we have been think (as ex nihilo sources) they must be functioning as repositories and conduits distributing responsibility across populations.

The notion of distributed responsibility not only promises to make sense, at least schematically, of the moral landscape, it addresses the crisis of vanishing accountability implicit in urbanization and specialization. As well, it is scalable and able to encompass good and bad consequences emanating from corporate and national agendas.

Finally, perhaps most importantly, the idea of distributed responsibility empowers individuals who can now see themselves as repositories and conduits for

> *Mens rea* accounts are increasingly inadequate in the context of specialized occupations and micro-moralists.

malignant and excellent moral assets. They come to see that they did not author these assets. They were imbibed, inculcated, assimilated ... during gestation and exacerbated or nurtured thereafter. This means individuals can leave off figuring out who is to be blamed and get to work identifying and repairing complicities with the alacrity one who discovers a cancerous growth is interested in seeking it out and getting rid of it.

To use a more pleasant metaphor, if the boat keeping one alive is sinking, fussing about who is to blame is not nearly as useful as identifying and fixing problems, and bailing furiously while doing so.

ᎣᏈᎯᏈᎯᏈᎯ

The notion of distributed responsibility[8] has another relevance. Mens rea explanations are increasingly

---

8   Floridi L. 2016 Faultless Responsibility: on the nature and allocation of moral responsibility for distributed moral actions. *Phil. Trans. R. Soc. A*374: 20160112

unconvincing as human beings take up specialized occupations and become micro-moralists. To the extent that granular notions of responsibility are the root of problems, to the extent that we cannot all be bystanders or victims, a corner will have been turned.

ማጐ.ማጐ.ማጐ.

In the face of logical difficulties and toxic consequences, why have societies been reluctant to acknowledge that person-hood is not innate?

An important reason is that the notion of automatically-occurring person-hood tidies up moral bookkeeping, rationalizes meritocracies and sanctions inequities. When individuals are deemed the authors of everything going on, saints and sinners can be organized, rewarded and punished without further ado. More importantly, everyone else gets to live childish, irresponsible lives.

This subterfuge has deep roots. Talking about birthdays nine months after conception encourages fantasies about incarnated souls, raises the possibility of surviving death and sets the stage for suicide bombers enjoying heavenly trysts with eager virgins.

Another benefit is so important that it has become instinctive: Once puberty has occurred and adults are born, they get to regard every notion that occurs to them as perfect, every inclination as legitimate. They get to put their 'best feats' forward without hesitation or discussion.

Progress and Development

There is a dark side of course. Adults' mutual hostility, granular focus, micro-moral, micro-rational spheres of engagement ... creates opportunities for political and economic mischief. Institutions, corporations, wealthy agendas ... flourish when adults refuse to talk among themselves with a view to figuring out what is going on and organizing push-backs if necessary.

In 1988, Edward Herman and Noam Chomsky described the results in the book Manufacturing Consent:

> Democracy in America is not functioning in an ideal sense but more in the sense that Lippmann noted in Public Opinion (where a specialized class of about 20 percent of the people—but who are also a target of propaganda—manages democratic functioning) and, in effect, are under control of a power elite, who more or less own the institutions. The masses of people (80 percent) are marginalized, diverted and controlled by what he calls Necessary Illusions.[9]

These 'necessary illusions' include complacency that government and commercial activities are adequately scrutinized by cognoscenti and investigative journalism. Indeed, thanks to the INTERNET, social media, Facebook ... more pundits and experts than the world has ever seen are now talking day and night on the public's behalf.

---

9   http://hope.journ.wwu.edu/tpilgrim/j190/
    Chomsky.summary.html

Unfortunately, outsourcing thinking and talking (to comedians and cognoscenti) reduces the likelihood that people understand that they have skin and complicity in the game. Refugee populations and climate change threats provide pundits with work that never seems to make a difference. Nations that provide people like David Suzuki, Al Gore, Noam Chomsky ... with pulpits are often pursuing economic and political agendas implicated in the problems public intellectuals bring to public attention. Nations encouraging such discussions have better credentials than those who do not. Noam Chomsky has been making a case that the USA is the world's premier state terrorist, even as the fact that the USA is hosting his indefatigable efforts challenges his arguments.

I do not suggest Professor Chomsky has *mens rea* complicity in this outcome. Chomsky believes human beings are moral and rational agents, consciously fashioning and communicating understandings. Disciplined, palpable outrage animates *The Manufacture of Consent* Chomsky and Edward S Herman wrote in 1988:[10] The underlying logic is simple: Individuals capable of the linguistic miracles Chomsky's work describes—but who behave myopically in their private lives and political choices—must have been suborned by duplicitous governments, media interests and the industrial complex.

---

10 https://en.wikipedia.org/wiki/Manufacturing_Consent

Progress and Development

The notion of distributed responsibility, with persons as repositories and conduits of unfortunate proceedings, puts problems in a different light—and distributes possible repairs across populations. If even a significant portion of populations

> The capacity to generate and experience toy world events distinguishes human beings.

identified and repaired innocent complicities many problems would disappear.

ᎣᎴ.ᎣᎴ.ᎣᎴ.

As Illustration 1 demonstrates, for almost a century western populations have not been having enough children to replace themselves. This failure of the most important of subsistence activities is rooted in notions of innate person-hood. If I am incarnated (or highly-evolved) I am not really of this place and can double down on my personal agendas. In urban circumstances, this means that, because children are demanding, expensive and optional, many are choosing to have one child, or none at all.

Since modern economies must grow or collapse, next generations must be imported, and this means destabilized, impoverished third world populations guarantee large populations of would-be immigrants to select from.

The notion of innate person-hood has other unfortunate consequences:

1. Institutions, nations, corporations, leader/follow forms of life ... depend upon the naivete that comes from claiming person-hood as a birthright. If nothing prevents human beings from becoming persons, then why not develop everything so persons will have improved options and pleasures?

2. Religions, especially monotheistic religions, depend upon the idea that human beings become

    > Human beings instinctively embrace leader/follower relationships.

    persons supernaturally, i.e., by being incarnated. The world is not our only or final home, indeed it is nothing more than a phase to be negotiated en route to Heaven or Hell.

3. The notion that consciousness does stuff does not capture everything meant by persons, but is the hinge exceptionalism claims depend upon. This is where human beings get to stipulate that other creatures are not morally relevant. They may be aware of what is going on, but they are not aware that they are aware! Even *they* is generous on our part, a patronizing anthropomorphism. This is why we do not think other creatures treat one another well or badly. Only persons can behave immorally.

4. Even here we have a bolt hole: human beings must be conscious before guilty mind tests can be applied.

Progress and Development

5. We are also flexible about which human beings qualify as persons. Pro-choicers believe fetuses within two trimesters of conception can be aborted: not yet conscious, they are not yet persons.

6. Equally facile calculations occupy pro-lifers. They are concerned about toxic insults to fetuses (no alcohol during pregnancy), but indifferent to well-being after birth, especially the well-being of distant populations.

7. Birthdays can be understood as dissolving obligations to provide wholesome circumstances.

መኮ፡መኮ፡መኮ፡

The idea that human beings experience two stages of gestation before puberty/birth invites another question. If embryology recapitulates ontogeny (as depicted in Illustration 3), could a parallel cultural recapitulation be a critical component of person-hood?

A good deal of physiological and neurological development occurs during infancy and childhood. Until recently, much of this occurred in communities engaged in subsistence activities. These circumstances and experiences have been obliterated in wealthy nations and bastardized in impoverished ones. One feature of human life has not changed however. Human beings continue to organize into leader/follower hierarchies. This was essential when human beings arrived helpless in the world nine months after conception. The problem is, seminal subsistence experiences have been outsourced and instinctive responses amplified, institutionalized and commercialized. Of course, they are also continuing within families, to the extent that family life remains. Combined, these

> Persons are keen to talk and have no idea of how conversations will proceed until they hear what they are saying. This does not bother them at all.

circumstances are dangerous in ways human beings have no instinctive way of identifying or defending against.

Whatever persons amount to, the capacity to be self-initiating and governing must be a core element. This self-sufficiency includes physiological, psychological and economic components. These achievements must begin during external gestation.

At the end of internal gestation, human beings move from womb to world. They start breathing, eating, moving, defecating ... for themselves. The urgent need is to become self-sufficient and self-sustaining. This is why children are insatiably active and curious: They are transforming food into robust bodies. They are sampling, tasting, experimenting with ... the world around them. Puberty, the aggressive moral paralysis of adulthood, is looming. The fitness of genetic legacies and epigenetic circumstances will be put to the test. Cram as much in as possible, batten down one's hatches and make a run for it.

Progress and Development

Progress or Persons

Human beings invest cultural and technological resources in security and creature comfort projects, and this is usually a good idea. However, ten thousand years ago, a threshold was crossed and unintended consequences began undermining up front benefits. Typically, these harms were hidden beneath immediate gains. For example, money, financial institutions and surveyors spawned nations, plots of land and lots of plots.

Several thousand years later, urbanization and globalization rule the world and rue out days. We are at a juncture where the narrative can turn out wonderfully or badly:

- We can continue to make external gestation experiences replicate internal. Children will be born into the world, but the differences between internal and external wombs will become even more imperceptible.

- Alternatively, cultural and technological resources could make leader/follower forms of life obsolete. The human beings: persons ratio could move towards 1:1 rather than 1:0.

To get a clearer idea of what is at stake, it is necessary to say something about consciousness and subjectivity. Subjectivity is our sense of being someone and knowing it. Without subjectivity, nothing matters. Pointing this out would be nothing more than a tedious truism if consciousness really was, as we have been assuming, innate and automatic. Consciousness would exist no matter what we get up to or fail to get up to. However, if Derek Parfit is correct and consciousness is the result of stringing conscious episodes together, the story is different. Conscious episodes are not innate—that is what episodes means! They occur when there is a need to get complicated information on internal cognitive blackboards, define projects that require moments or weeks to achieve or involve collaborations with other human beings.

The question is: What happens if human beings are reduced to functionaries: soldiers, workers, consumers, fans ... behaving in ways that never require conscious episodes? What happens when human beings' capacity to generate conscious episodes is co-opted and becomes corporate or government assets accessible via smartphones and other technologies? What if human beings have been organizing, automating, outsourcing ... their sense of being alive out of existence?

Is this hyperbole or a real threat? When individuals are responding to conversations, novel events, sirens, telephone calls or some insight within, conscious episodes launder such events into lived experiences that participate in further cognitive events and, externally, as conversations and activities. Consciousness does not author these proceedings, it registers them as lived experiences so they participate in further cognitive events in the same way actual, external events participate. (See Double Boiler Cartoon at end.)

Since this means there is no overarching, innate consciousness, we have no way of noticing when conscious episodes are not occurring. Like the proverbial frog, we can be boiled alive—or rendered unaware of the lack of internally-sourced intents and purposes—if the origin and state of our being is adjusted slowly enough.

To make modern circumstances even more seductive and existentially perilous, conscious episodes regularly participate in further conscious episodes, and we think thinking is going on and that we are *doing* this thinking. Not so. Conscious episodes are not being generated and then appended to existing memories by innate consciousness. They are generated by intrinsically active memory elements or micro-dispositions. As introspection reveals, experiences, memories, skills ... participate automatically in responses to external events. These elements are evoked by events and generate further conscious episodes. This is how conversations happen, narratives continue and a sense of identity and subjectivity emerges.

There is another way of coming to this conclusion. Human beings can only become aware of events, including cognitive events, after they have occurred. The contents of awareness must either exist prior to conscious episodes featuring them or they must be generated by the cognitive events achieving awareness. It makes sense to think of human cognition in terms of cascading conditioned responses identical to those common in other forms of life. Conditioned responses are triggered by conditioned stimuli and occur spontaneously. In human stories, an enormous depth of conditioned responses are laid down during external gestation. They are exquisitely tuned to local circumstances and so filtering and evoking mechanisms automatically integrate human beings with their native circumstances. This explains our capacity to respond effortlessly and voluminously to external events and to the phenomenal objects/events comprising our subjective lives. Again, a principal function of conscious episodes is to allow cognitive activities to participate in further cognitive events just as if they were external experiences.

ᠤᠶᠤ.ᠤᠶᠤ.ᠤᠶᠤ.

This makes so much sense that one wonders how the idea of incarnated souls, innate persons or efficacious consciousness got going. A few possibilities have occurred to me:

- Leader/follower, rich/poor ... forms of life organize what is going on in ways human beings find seductive. Thinking about what is going on in terms of Gods, villains, victims, heroes ... makes inscrutable proceedings more manageable. God is at the top of the ladder. God-like human beings are perched one rung down. Other creatures are further down a ladder that disappears into the distance far below. Whether looking up or down, everything is arrayed for our pleasure and use.

Progress and Development

- These sanctions explain why human beings continue to embrace leader/follower forms of life, no matter how monstrous inequities of wealth and power become.

- These seductions help explain why subsistence economies are abandoned as soon as technologies permit. Getting to decide what to do with one's life is advertised as the best life possible, but there is no evidence that this is really what human beings want, and a great deal that we prefer to live in bondage and thralldom.

Given that cultural resources and technologies now make self-sufficiency and freedom universally possible, how else to explain why is there so little interest?

Ayes Everywhere

Pens are not mightier than swords. Pens are, however, implicated in the uses swords are put to. As a metaphor for reading and writing, pens are engines of cultural and technological achievement and a core element determining whether human beings become persons.

When all goes well, enlarged spheres of understanding and technologies diminish the need for

> Whether occupations are mundane or exotic, specialists are morally and rationally paralyzed.

leader/follower arrangements. However, these same achievements can be invested in murdering or partially aborting human beings.

From the point of view of nations and corporations, the partially-aborted are preferable because they become reliable value-generating assets. Business plans depend upon workers and consumers far more than unruly persons. For corporations and nations, persons are more trouble than they are worth. Accordingly, the best thing is ensure that as few as possible turn up.

In addition, the partially aborted often have robust wants, needs and skills that can be assembled into organizations of any size or complexity. If leaders do not step up to do this work (rarely a problem), the partially-aborted will often

Progress and Development

thresh around until a fortuitous organization catches fire and gives them work to do.

If this seems fanciful, we need to remember that human beings who do not become persons have plenty of reasons to seek out and link up with similarly-truncated individuals. Solutions—often ugly—can sometimes be accomplished by forming into strength-in-numbers groups. Klu Klux Clans, Criminal gangs and, a recent invention, Incel (involuntarily celibate) groups.

However their genesis is understood, corporations, nations, religions, sects ... develop agendas with little interest in the well-being of the individuals comprising them.

Readers can test this with a thought experiment: We are all citizens of one nation or another. If we reflect upon what 'our nation' has been getting up to, it is immediately clear that this is distinct from what we intend for ourselves, or what we think 'our nation' should be getting up to.

Thus, I have no idea what Canada should get up to, but I have a clear sense that Canada is an entity, along with the USA, Russia, England and Australia. Other people doubtlessly have different lists. One thing that is common, I think, is that no one expects to be consulted about what their nation should get up to. Presumably this means nations and corporations get up to stuff that no citizen, employee or customer intends. The question of where corporate and national intentions come from is interesting and important.

The nature and scope of national projects, purposes, agendas ... cannot be predicted by summing or averaging the wishes of citizens. Canada has a robust democracy, but everything Canada does is more or less unsatisfactory to every citizen. This is not only because democracies proceed by averaging desires and values in ways that satisfy no one. Corporations and nations incorporate dozens, hundreds, millions ... of individuals into alien forms of life. From the resulting vantage points, these creatures pursue projects that do not, and could not, originate in workers', consumers' or citizens' conscious episodes.

Each of us is a living example of how this works. Your and my sense of being alive occurs outside of the spheres of the cells, neurons and physiological proceedings comprising our bodies. Our subjectivities emerge out of these proceedings. We are sums greater than, or at least unpredictable from, the activities of our parts.

I think this means that much of what is going on in the modern world reflects similarly emergent and hence non-human agendas. I think this means that corporations' and nations' projects are morally detached from workers, consumers and citizens. This is not new of course, although the proportion has never come so close to 100%.

As well, the agendas of partially-aborted human beings will be relatively granular, their sense of possibility and responsibility correspondingly minuscule. Big Picture worries and push-backs require persons who see themselves as self-sustaining and self-sufficient. Only such individuals expect to look after themselves and decide what to do out of their own resources. Only such individuals are likely to think about other human beings' well-being when disasters are not occurring.

For individuals who have achieved person-hood, patronizing corporations and governments, shopping malls and sports arenas ... are last resorts. For the half-aborted, they are the only option. This is why subsistence activities during 2nd gestation intervals are so important. Courses of experience that proceed directly from wombs to urbanized, specialized lives are toxic, no matter how boisterously Kim Jong-un welcomes unemployed nuclear engineers and physicists from the USSR.

I do not suggest that specialized occupations are verboten. It is possible for persons to become nuclear engineers, perhaps even in beneficial ways. It is impossible for nuclear engineers to become persons—even if 11th hour epiphanies occur because they happened to glance at the Doomsday clock.

I refer to nuclear specialists because they are often in the news, and because it is especially important to get nuclear stuff right. However, no matter how mundane or exotic, specialists are all at risk of being co-opted and incorporated into activities whose consequences will never cross their minds. On the other hand, specialists who achieve person-hood before they became employees have vantage points from which corporations, nations and other bastard life forms could perhaps be harnessed and civilized.

ᎋᎋᎋ

Although social media platforms and the INTERNET are busy, busy, busy, many are worried that public awareness is collapsing into a version of the pre-reflective stupor described by Jean Paul Sartre in *Being and Nothingness*[11]. What is pre-reflective awareness? Sartre's example involves the feeling one sometimes has of footsteps in rooms above, but ignore because they have nothing to do with what one has in mind.

At the same time, it is possible to imagine circumstances wherein the same footsteps would be trigger conscious episodes and vigorous responses. Suppose someone had reason to believe that someone else was planning to steal the family silverware? The point is that the meaning of sensory information—in fact whether it has any meaning—is determined by agendas individuals happen to have.

This begs a question: What if individuals are not getting up to anything that could be tracked back to internal proceedings? Intuitively and anecdotally, we are frenetically busy these days, but still might not be getting up to anything that counts as an internally-conceived project! What if our activities are all responses to sports, media events, video games, music, responding to texts ...? What if our conscious

---

11 http://www.iep.utm.edu/sartre-ex/

Progress and Development

episodes are stitching into subjectivities and notions of being alive—but every episode is externally triggered by other individuals, corporations or politicians? Would these episodes, and the subjectivities they give rise to, count as persons?

If *persons* is to retain any interesting meaning, the answer has to be no. Nothing prevents externally-sourced conscious episodes from melding into narratives supporting the false appearance of moral agent-hood. Nothing prevents de facto brains in vats from having experiences wherein they seem to themselves to be engaging with actual people in an actual world, curating and editing information and making responses.

Au contraire, mon ami! Such claims are the provenance of human beings at least occasionally initiating and harvesting original projects. Such claims are the provenance of persons.

Self-Determination

Human narratives will always be explicable in terms of genetics, gestation experiences and current events. If external gestation includes subsistence activities, if we have the broad margins Henry Thoreau recommended, these ingredients will digest one another's significance, generate insights, conversations and actions that would not have otherwise occurred.

This is why the path to person-hood provides a way—I think the only way—to evade the constraints of causality, determinism and behaviourism. Cognitive events will remain explicable (even if researchers have not solved every puzzle), but human beings who become persons will embody 'home grown' proceedings that are *theirs and theirs alone.*

The sense of loss involved giving up supernatural fantasies about conscious agency is more than compensated for by cultivating subsistence activities into moral and rational self-determination.

The following sketch hints that human beings may have more self-determining resources beavering away than we thought.

How Conversations Happen

I recently had a conversation with a young woman about one of my hobbyhorse topics. I did not expect the conversation to last, but she seemed interested, poking back, not looking for an 'avenue of egress'.

This is so rare that I did not know how to behave.

In any case, I was rescued by another woman, obviously acquainted with the person I had been talking to. She interrupted us, speaking at half-volume.

When I realized what was happening, I apologized for interrupting her. At this point, something interesting happened. She was clearly unaware that she had crashed our conversation. As soon as she realized, she was embarrassed.

Both discussions collapsed. After a few moments, I found a reason to leave and left them to their own devices.

The incident reminded me of a similar experience years earlier. I occasionally visited a family that loved to talk. They were delightfully, irrepressibly, voluminously garrulous. Whether over lunch, dinner or an evening's entertainment, whenever they were in one another's company, mother, father and daughter talked simultaneously and constantly.

As far as I could tell, I was the only one listening.

Occasionally, to my amazement, one of them would think of something that was apparently off-topic—although the topic was rarely obvious. This individual would scribble and pass a note to one of the others, under the flow of the conversation so to speak.

I did not understand what was going on then, but have since developed a theory: Communications were occurring among their respective 'cognitive stew pots'. These communications that were occurring outside of the conscious episodes of anyone at the table.

As well, these communications seemed to reflect ruminations that had gone on in each of them since they last shared a meal. These results were now being communicated without being funnelled through anyone's conscious episodes.

Such communications may reflect the way information was shared before notions of self, agency, morality ... necked conversations down to a trickle.

This could be more common than we think. The woman who interrupted my conversation may have been utilizing a communication model unimpeded by the need for individuals to pay conscious attention or wait for breaks in conversations.

ᎋ.ᎋ.ᎋ.

Human beings have two digestive systems, the one referred to as the alimentary or standard digestive system and the one called the brain.

Progress and Development

The standard digestive system does almost all of its work outside of awareness. The only time conscious episodes are involved is when ruminating has run its course. Peristalsis occurs and a conscious episode ensures that results are properly integrated with world.

Conscious episodes serve analogous purposes in the second ruminating system. Ideas, notions, responses ... pop into awareness so they can be integrated with external events or held back because individuals understand that venting is not acceptable right then, or perhaps not at all.

This may explain why we sometimes say: "What's cooking?", "Simmer Down!", "Put a lid on it!"

ᴓᕈ.ᴓᕈ.ᴓᕈ.

For thousands of years, human beings have assumed that conversations involve conscious agents talking to one another about what was going on *out there*. We assumed that at least some aspects of our lives are under our conscious control, perhaps after consulting cultural recommendations and conversations, perhaps because of malignant choices.

We have been blaming and praising one another because we believe that consciousness curates information, considers experiences and then injects choices into what is going on. Unlike lesser creatures—whose behaviour is completely predictable given enough information—we believe that we *conduct ourselves* by virtue of the fact that we are conscious.

We like it that this consciousness is mysterious because this means we get to talk about being incarnated souls or evolution's finest flower. The notion of incarnated souls is especially popular because it positions individuals to talk about what is going on, judge people's judgments and maybe, just maybe, get out of Dodge alive.

In preliterate cultures, in addition to talking to one another, human beings spent a lot of time communicating with their unconscious brains. [12] We still do this while dreaming but it seems likely that early human beings dreamed day and night. In the daytime, dreams involved waking experiences involved forest gods, rain gods, household gods .... These hallucinations passed suggestions and ideas from the non-dominant stew-pot to the executive boiler.

After thousands of years, our growing sense of exceptionalism and self-referential awareness required moving beyond Pantheism to one Almighty God. An omniscient, omnipotent being was needed to explain the creation of such exceptional beings, provide Heaven and Hell so life made sense, and occasionally interrupt the natural order on our behalf if we were sufficiently obsequious.

---

12 Julian Jaynes, *The Origins of Consciousness in the Breakdown of the Bi-Cameral Mind,* www.julianjaynes.org

Progress and Development

The problem is that several cultures came to the same conclusion and launched their own Almighty God. Since there can only be one Supreme Being, billions of armed to the teeth human beings now find themselves glaring at one another.

Even if this does not cause us to blow everything to smithereens, exceptional human beings with God on their side are dangerous for environmental reasons. They regard the world as a trysting place, a vale of tears, a stopover on the way to Heaven. There is no reason to worry whether human beings are responsible for the Anthropocene. Other creatures exist for our use and amusement. Evolutionists see other forms of life in similarly utilitarian terms: They are valuable if their is a market for them. They are interesting if they illuminate how human beings became exceptional. Sophisticated individuals recognize the importance of a healthy biosphere, but that is still in terms of what is good for us.

Most human beings are faithful and, by definition, do not care about the world. If we are resolutely faithful, we would rather blow everything up than let infidels prevail. Moreover, the faithful cannot really murder people in the sense of terminating their existence. Killing someone only moves them along to meet their Maker and give an account of themselves.

Consequences are symptoms not causes. This is why getting to the root of problems is necessary before repairs are possible. The idea that consciousness is innate and can create and act upon its contents is one such diagnosis.

Another dangerous fantasy is the idea that ideas can be passed among persons using consciousness as both a conduit and judging faculty.

Even if this was true, the commonsense notion of communication and conversation is impossible. Children are in no position to make judgments and adults instinctively reject information that does not resemble the information that made them the adults they are.

We also err when we think the world is proceeding along dark paths because individuals have been leveraging Mother Tongues, cultural resources and technologies and making in conscious—and therefore indictable—choices from these vantage points. The deep problem is that we see ourselves as conscious agents situated outside of what is going on. The reality is that we are perched on giant cultural shoulders and rushing pall-mall along development road. We think this is excellent because we get occasional glimpses of scenery rushing by and assume that we are in control.

These fantasies have also been causing us to overlook filling one another's stew-pots with wholesome ingredients. Then,

Progress and Development

as troubles pile up, we make scapegoats of one another using *conscious agency* as a one-size-fits-all rationale?[13]

ᎣᎩᎬᎣᎩᎬᎣᎩᎬ

Suppose a human being has completed *internal gestation* and been delivered (i.e., born) into the world. At this point, *external gestation* commences. For the next dozen years, this being will grow and develop. Prolonged gestation is necessary to develop big-brained, fragile human beings to the point that survival becomes possible.

Since birth occurs at the end of gestation, human birthdays coincide with puberty. For those who like to keep score, we are all ten or twelve years younger than we thought, but have fewer years to live.

At puberty, human beings have developed to a state of independence comparable to other species' newborns shortly after birth. This prolonged gestation is necessary so human beings' big brains can develop in the context of cultural and social experiences.

Human beings can be thought of as whatever is going on within containers or sacks initially defined by skins. These containers enlarge as cultural resources and experiences are internalized. No matter how large or small they become, these containers generate adults' sense of themselves. This is why claims of adequacy and competence are defended as

---

13 These possibilities were introduced in *Modern Problems* and further explored in *Diaspora or Oblivion*.

fiercely as body parts. The people and circumstances constituting one's childhood are suffused with meaning and poignancy. Everything thereafter is assimilated or repudiated according to whether it lines up with these experiences.

This process is accelerated by naming individuals as soon as internal gestation is complete. This helps children get to know one another and make plans beyond here and now encounters. Names help human beings think of themselves as *selves*.

Being identifiable makes re-identifiability possible, and so we remember that we came across one another previously. These experiences set the stage for talk about *realism*. Time and space must exist to explain where people are hanging their hats when not in one another's company.

ᙢᙢᙢ

The characteristic of containers that makes living organisms possible is semi-permeability: nutrients flow in and are contained until they render one another's value. During ' external gestation, nutrient flows increase, often to the consternation of care-givers. In similar fashion, information flows in. Children thrum with energy, they charge around harvesting experiences as if their lives depended upon it.

At puberty this semi-permeable sack membrane reverses direction and starts restricting information. The only stimuli now given a pass are those that are congruent with those

Progress and Development

internalized during gestation. This is when it makes sense to say that human beings have been born.

Henceforth adults must manage with what has been absorbed. Contradictory information is reflexively dismissed.[14] Ambiguous information is sorted into acceptable and unacceptable piles for further processing. Information now deemed unacceptable is usually deprecated or denigrated so its dismissal appears intelligible.

These dismissals are not moral or rational failures even if the information dismissed is life-saving. The need to reduce computational burdens and response times is the reason biases, prejudices and bigotries exist. (All right, they also feel good!)

Re-framing gestation, puberty and birth-dates links adults' hostility to new ideas and people with new ideas to an important adaptation. No matter what species is involved, adults need to stop learning and growing and get on with it.

This also explains how evolution has been selecting for genetic and cultural excellence. Adult human beings must become defensive and close-minded so the fitness of particular combinations genetic and cultural inheritances can be tested.

However, this is not good news for environmental and peace-making projects that depend upon human beings sharing and acting upon understandings and concerns.

_____

14 See: Permissible cognitive dissonance.

Indeed, this recalcitrance and mutual hostility seems certain to worsen. As societies become increasingly complex, dependent and specialized, the incidence of ambiguous—or completely inscrutable—information is rising. Indeed, since the sum total of information is said to be doubling yearly (if not monthly), biases, prejudices and bigotries seem certain to increase.

ጥ፡ጥ፡ጥ፡

We can explain the conversational prowess of the family described earlier with a simple story: Adult human beings are crammed with experiences and cultural resources. These assets comprise the extended phenotypes educated, socialized, cultured men and women understand themselves to consist of. People do not think of themselves in terms of bodies alone but as compilations of bodies, experiences, skills, tools in workshops and sewing supplies.

These resources are not waiting to be acted upon by conscious faculties. They are boiling around, digesting one another's significance, generating insights, flashes of inspiration, puns, dreams, good and bad ideas and projects to undertake. Memories and other cognitive resources are interrupted responses seeking satisfaction. Hence they constantly invoke and evoke one another—this is perhaps clearest when we dream, but we dream day and night. When we are awake dream events integrate seamlessly with local events and we call this thinking about what is going on. This evoking, this dreaming, continues until we actually do something, or, more often these days, send someone a text or make a call to relieve the pressure, to vent.

If these proceedings are organic in the sense of being face-to-face, human beings are in touch through sense organs as well as language abilities. This means spontaneously communicating at several levels. Usually, but not always, these communications involve conscious episodes.

This boiling around also explains why people break into conversation (and sometimes into conversations!) at every opportunity. We are like sea gulls when someone throws french fries on a beach. We have no idea what we will say or do until we notice ourselves saying and doing stuff."

Any other explanation involves supernatural stories and fairy tails, and we know where that leads.

ᎣᏊ.ᎣᏊ.ᎣᏊ.

Cognitive filters (de facto immune systems) defend against ideas, experiences and conversations lying outside notions of what is valuable and true internalized during gestation. These filters operate automatically because they are patterned upon conditioned responses. Their function is to protect against conscious episodes that could dilute or contradict understandings acquired before puberty. This preemptive function is important because conscious episodes allow cognitive events to be experienced as if they were external. Protecting the integrity of bodies of experiences and understandings is as important to adult human beings as protecting body parts is to non-human forms of life.

In other words, adult human beings are faithful to experiences internalized during childhood. All religions and political dogmatisms are patterned upon the sanctity of childhood experiences.

ᎣᏏᎣᏏᎣᏏ

How is the filtering protecting gestational experiences accomplished? Internalized information functions as template and programming for filtering mechanisms. These mechanisms operate automatically and unconsciously— which is why the family anecdote above is significant. Communications among a small cadre of trusted others were occurring subliminally.

Generally, individuals take one another's measure before consenting to have conscious experiences with them. Such communications assess whether individuals are safe candidates to talk to; which is to say, whether they can be trusted to not say contentious or provocative stuff that would compromise one's extended phenotype.

We experience versions of this sorting out all the time. Before a word is said, we assess whether individuals are likely to threaten the coherence of our beliefs and values. If they seem benign—congruent, consonant, homogeneous— we are willing, if not eager, to talk until the cows come home.

Progress and Development

If this assessment turns out to be wrong and conversations turn bad—if someone brings up animal welfare or factory farms during a steak dinner—conversations stiffen up and future invite lists are unconsciously adjusted.

In similarly unconscious ways, populations sort into Us vs. Them and Leader/Follower arrangements.[15] These arrangements then organize populations into gangs, platoons, congregations and political parties.

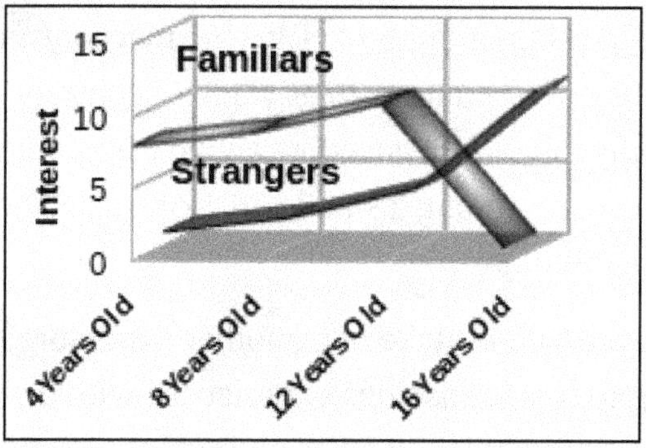

This is my depiction of the interest patterns associated with gestation and puberty that underlie these events.

Political and economic hazards lurk in the post-puberty falling off of interest in familiars. Leader/follower relationships are now rooting up in earnest, the difference

15 Leader/follower relationships occur instinctively. Like external gestation, such arrangements are necessary to achieve the results human beings' big brains make possible.

being that allegiance is transferred from familiars to strangers. The only stipulation is that leaders must resonate with values and priorities internalized during external gestation. To take a current example, Donald Trump's supporters have Trump-style values and are similarly resistant to discussing these values' credentials.

However, it is not the case that adults consciously choose to be leaders or followers. Moreover, they are not choosing which ideas will be entertained. Unsatisfactory ideas simply do not get past immune systems and so never participate in conscious episodes. Such preemptive filtering is not restricted to right wing populations. Left-wing, centrist and religious ideologues cleave just as fiercely to distinctive principles.

ᎣᏛᎣᏛᎣᏛ

There is a related phenomenon feeding into the moral and rational paralysis afflicting public life everywhere. Individual exist in networks of familiar people. Although everything seems friendly, the reality is that *familiars* have brittle relationships. Things only go smoothly only as long as mutual circumstances and values are honoured. Thus, Catholics, Protestants, Muslims ... must remain faithful to the understandings that spawned them or risk being ostracized. If this cannot be managed, indiscretions should be kept under hats. Full-throated doctrinal debates are not an option, while get-together celebrations and family history websites are just what the doctor ordered.

Progress and Development

The irony is that adults perceive familiars as doubly threatening if they go rogue and start questioning fundamental understandings. Since, by definition, familiars are hard to ignore, deviants must therefore be summarily dealt with. This result is local moral and rational paralysis. Substantive issues and over-arching concerns cannot be discussed with familiars and so families and communities are stymied.

The result—people who know each other rarely consult with one another about what to do about substantive issues—is good news for those on the upside of inequities. Leader/follower relationships made good sense when the world was young, communities needed to deploy all their resources and nothing much could be done beyond eking out a living.

A Solution

The Human Development Index (seen above and duplicated below) demonstrates that hunters and gatherers and agrarian populations tend to have large families. If these children survive and reproduce, extra mouths mean families continue in marginal circumstances. Historically, this has led to unsustainable population growth and other Malthusian dilemmas.

Populations that are better off—mostly urbanized post Industrial Revolution families—face a different problem. They have been responding to prosperity by having fewer children. As the graph shows, fertility rates fall below stable population levels when the Human Development Index rises to .8. This was clear in 1975 and even more pronounced in 2005.

In these circumstances, the benefits of technologies and industrialization are invested in life-style improvements, passed to wealthy individuals or reflect the overhead burden children represent in urban circumstances. The remainder of these benefits is being spent on corporate competition for consumer dollars and military expenditures protecting the resulting wealthy class from disgruntled poor populations.

This is an an ironic state of affairs. Populations with fertility rates below 2.1 children per woman (2.4 in poor nations) are not replacing themselves. They are engaging in self-administered genocide—a never before seen consequence of

Progress and Development

prosperity. In addition, this is politically unstable. Wealthy
nations need immigrants because modern economies must
grow or collapse. This means the world economy needs to
be inequitable so poor populations are anxious to leave
home to seek their fortune.

What's the answer? The Human Development index

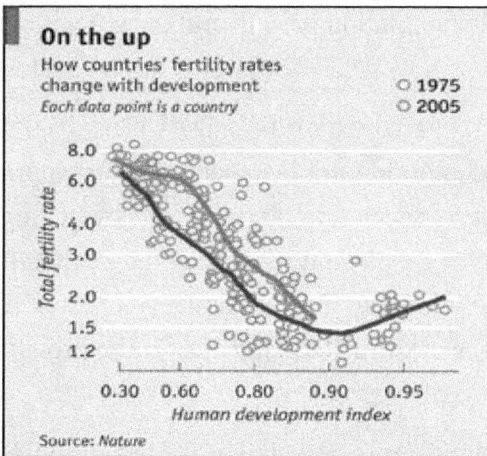

On the up

How countries' fertility rates
change with development   ○ 1975
Each data point is a country   ○ 2005

Total fertility rate (vertical axis): 8.0, 6.0, 4.0, 3.0, 2.0, 1.5, 1.2

Human development index (horizontal axis): 0.30, 0.60, 0.80, 0.90, 0.95

Source: *Nature*

suggests a solution. When the index passes .90, fertility rates
move upward. It is reasonable to suppose that sustainable
populations could be achieved and that increases to general
well-being is the way to do so.

How can the Human Development Index be moved further
along when the planet cannot sustain present levels of
prosperity?

This is where possibilities converge! Local economies, in
tandem with central economies, could retrieve the economic,
social and psychological benefits of subsistence activities.

Such economies could root up everywhere. They would improve global well-being and stabilize national populations at replacement levels.

This could be important for an unexpected reason. In *Empty Planet,* Darrell Bricker and John Ibbitson argue that the human population is about to decline precipitously—a prediction implicit in the Human Development Index.

> We do not face the prospect of a population bomb but a population bust—a relentless, generation after generation culling of the human herd. ... Urbanization and the empowerment of women are having the same effect on developing countries as they had on developed countries. ... Across the planet, birth rates are plunging.[16]

Boom or bust, population patterns disengaged from natural constraints are bad news. The move to urbanization and specialization, that promised to eliminate the hardship of subsistence and agrarian cultures, opened a Pandora's box of troubles. A better path would have utilized technologies to improve subsistence activities, not obliterate them.

---

16 Darrell Bricker, John Ibbitson, *Empty Planet*(New York: Crown publishing, 2019) p.29.

On-Demand Economies

For decades I have been urging people to network and organize their requirements for goods and services so they can negotiate with suppliers and retailers as groups on more or less level playing fields.

What a straightforward way to make competition work and encourage local economies!

To my surprise—even though the production of goods and services is increasingly monopolistic—few seem interested.

Perhaps shopping spontaneously, without asking anyone's permission, is the only human activity we still get up to.

Perhaps such an obvious repair to important problems is too embarrassing to contemplate.

Whatever is going on, adults' hostility towards talking to and networking with people they know is obstructing their ability to repudiate leaders, corporations and the wealthy class. Not only are modern consumers dealing with massive corporations one by one, they are completely exposed to being messed with. Since we moved to cities and abandoned subsistence alternatives, we have to get our wallets out every time a want or need turns up.

In spite of my dismal track record, I want to again raise the idea of organized shopping. A new understanding of how dangerous the gap between producing and consuming is has occurred to me: Along with financial, equity and environmental consequences, global supply systems and fragmented consumers are having toxic consequences for person-hood and morality.

If this seems melodramatic, it is worth reminding ourselves that human beings are not incarnated little Gods or evolutionary miracles with innate person-hood. Person-hood may or may not be achieved. Person-hood requires genetic and cultural legacies interacting in precarious, complicated ways. Each is necessary for a good outcome, neither is necessary and sufficient

The good news is that the synergies required to spawn persons and moral possibilities are contained in subsistence activities. With cultural elements helping out, subsistence activities illuminate the ways individual and community well-being depend upon tightly-integrated producing and consuming activities. Subsistence activities involve producing valuable stuff (by hunting, working gardening ...) and consuming the fruits of these activities with as little waste as possible.

Every other creature manages this effortlessly. Whatever is caught or dug up is consumed without advertising, transportation, licensing or surveillance. Only human beings get up to complicated stuff producing, selling and consuming goods and services. The history of mankind can be organized under this heading.

Progress and Development

I am not making a Luddite argument. There is nothing wrong with figuring out ways do things efficiently or with less effort. However, these developments are toxic unless the benefits of new inventions and efficiencies are widely enjoyed.

We now have stupendous production capabilities, but much of the value created is wasted in spurious competitions, siphoned upstairs to wealthy populations or invested in security measures.

Subsistence activities and communities have an even more important function. Seeing that well-being is maximized by the most efficient path between production and consumption does not preclude co-operating with others to achieve economies of scale and strength-in-numbers benefits. The moral connection is that subsistence activities engaged in by communities centre upon whole persons, not individuals split into workers or shoppers. Every moral possibility depends upon having such experiences. Everything going south these days can be tracked back to the obliteration of communities and subsistence activities.

ᐊᖅᐊᖅᐊᖅ

A structural imbalance has been driving economies into dangerous waters. The results include inequities, social unrest and environmental crises. We have a sense of this, but seem powerless to resist its siren call. I refer to the steady drip of urbanization, centralization, economies of scale and the emergence of massively-capitalized corporations and global trade agreements.

These consequences cannot be repaired, or managed, by worrying about symptoms. To see a way forward, we need to go back to basics. Every economic theory considers human beings to be indivisible, immutable units—although debate continues about whether we are rational consumers or conscious, decision-making nodes trying to stay abreast of emergent, dynamic systems.

Most of the time this simple model makes sense. Every creature can be thought of as an organic capitalist: investing assets (bodies, energy, skills) in hunting, fishing, pecking, digging … activities, then consuming whatever has been achieved.

The thing to notice is that animals never have to find employment or advertise productive achievements. Although they can be thought of as 'shopping around' when looking for food (seeking value), animals do so as complete beings, not as shoppers brandishing money earned a day or a month earlier. Another lesson is that animals only seek food, water or shelter when they need to. The rule is: demand ▶ supply, not supply ▶ demand. As far as advertising, urbanization and dependency make possible, modern economies turn organic capitalism on its head and put supply elements in charge.

Progress and Development

The second benefit animals enjoy, and modern human beings can only envy, is that their producing and consuming activities are so integrated that middle-men, corporations or governments do not get a chance to colonize the space between getting and spending.

Of course, human beings are too smart to put up with subsistence life-styles. We have been figuring out faster, smarter and larger ways to do things. The problem is, we have been driving production efficiencies and ignoring the need to rationalize the other half of the supply-demand equation.

At the same time, we have been abandoning subsistence activities and self-reliant communities. These twinned blunders have been splitting individuals into workers and consumers who no longer think of themselves as integrated economic beings.

Lots of people have seen the dark side of the results, but almost always in ways focusing upon workers or consumers. Because we have a nostalgic belief that we are integrated individuals, we believe we are always optimizing our lives in whole person terms. Not so. We ponder difficulties we are having as workers. Later on, we worry about not having enough money to make ends meet.

In political terms, neo-liberals and conservatives focus upon supply-side issues, socialists and communists worry about distributed, egalitarian consumption.

The underlying collapse of whole-person understanding is the biggest consequence of the Industrial Revolution and the loss of subsistence life-styles or organic capitalism. Al Gore's *An Inconvenient Truth* foundered because he believed he was talking to whole persons and not to distressed workers or shoppers who needed to keep going down development road and damn the consequences. Although his efforts were well-received, they have had no discernible benefit in terms of global warming or resource depletion/pollution issues.

Another obstacle is that modern workers and consumers are unlikely to act upon even dire warnings. They have forgotten, or never developed, ways to put understandings into play that do not involve going to work or to the mall. Such capacities were commonplace in subsistence cultures and hybrid local/central economies until the middle of the 20th century.

Kate Raworth suggests another reason to be concerned about centralization and globalization:

> *If large-scale actors dominate an economic network by squeezing out the number and diversity of small and medium players, the results will be a highly unequal and brittle economy.*[17]

17 *Raworth, K.(2017) Doughnut Economics. (VT: Chelsea Green Publishing) p. 149.*

Progress and Development

The problem is that moral and rational analyses rarely include strategies individuals can implement in their own and one another's lives. These strategies should reward participants every step of the way, and they should be scalable.

This sounds like a tall order, but one possibility comes to mind.

Producers have been scaling up and consolidating into oligopolies and free trade agreements. The global economy and loss of national sovereignty are among the consequences. These proceedings are marginalizing or eliminating workers and rendering more and more consumers destitute.

Although comfortable and fun, blaming such difficulties upon corporations or politicians demoralizes and dis-empowers victims. Followers have been failing to organize their consuming needs as a way of pushing back against a now globally-organized supply system rewarding leaders. Even labour unions failed to seize this low-hanging fruit, a blunder bordering on malfeasance: If economies of scale and group negotiating make sense for producers and workers, do they not also make sense for consumers?

Grouped by tens or thousands, consumers could negotiate with retailers and manufacturers and make competition work. They could collate the recurring needs of group members and put out requests for tender on social media,

Amazon and Kijiji. Local economies could flourish. Local producers and artisans could enter into consignment contracts with retailers so there would be no need for retailers to purchase commodities. Instead they would take a commission on sales to compensate them for their investments. In this arrangement, suppliers would retrieve unsold goods in timely ways and reduce, for example, the need to discard perishables. By combining assets and investments in consignment arrangements, retailers and local suppliers could prosper and nurture local economies in the bargain.

In a thousand such ways, consumer groups could catalyze and benefit from the efficiencies and economies of scale producers have been enjoying. This would rationalize commercial waste and reduce environmental harms.

Even within urban settings, consumer groups would facilitate the local economic activities that once vitalized and stabilized communities. They would provide businesses with markets to pitch products and services to in low cost ways. Word of mouth and quality of goods and services would replace promotional torments.

Economies should be driven by the naturally-occurring requirements of human beings, not by the need of corporations to generate profit and not by lust of the wealthy to become still wealthier.

Progress and Development

Finally, individuals with whole person viewpoints would be resurrected—and empowered to do something about the mischief, economic and otherwise, going on.

HUMAN BEINGS
AS DOUBLE BOILERS

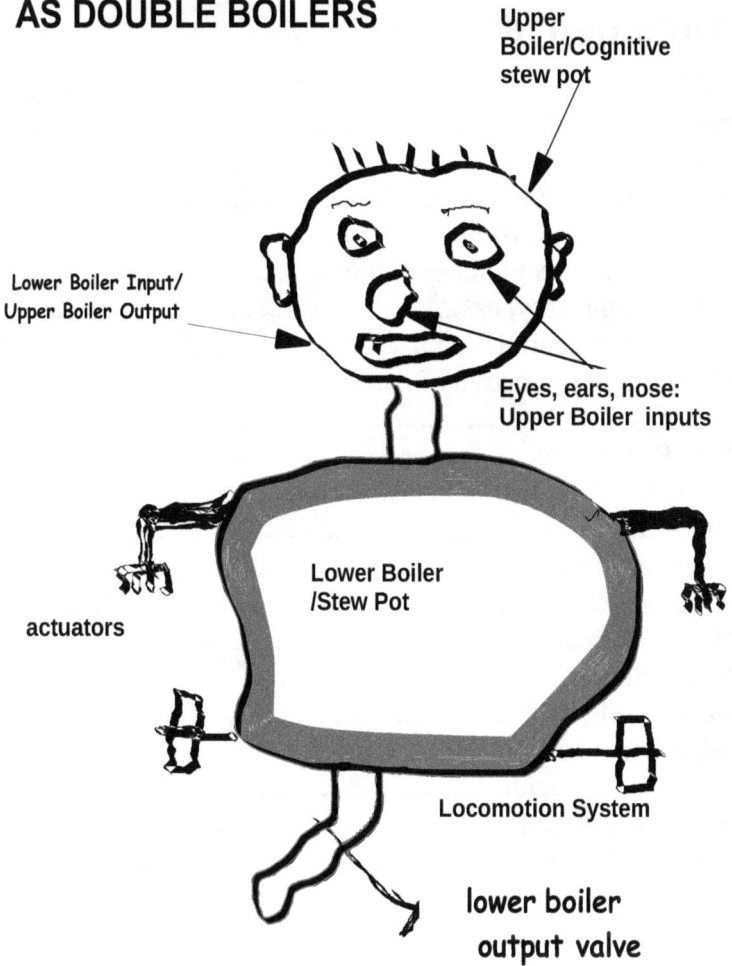

Upper Boiler/Cognitive stew pot

Lower Boiler Input/
Upper Boiler Output

Eyes, ears, nose:
Upper Boiler inputs

Lower Boiler
/Stew Pot

actuators

Locomotion System

lower boiler
output valve

Alphabetical Index

artificial intelligence..21
bastard life forms..49
Catholic Church...9
consciousness and subjectivity..40
distributed responsibility...32
embryology recapitulates ontogeny.....................................19
extended phenotypes...17
Haeckel's recapitulation..20
identity and subjectivity..42
incarnated souls..33, 55
Jean Paul Sartre..49
leader/follower hierarchies..38
let infidels prevail..56
mens rea episodes...13
narratives..42
Noam Chomsky...35
Partial abortions...25
standard digestive system..54
subsistence economies...44
voluntary genocide..8
 elongated gestation..22
"Simmer Down!...54

Resources:

- *Modern Problems, Ancient Perspectives;*
- *How Philosophy Could Save the World;*
- *Diaspora or Oblivion* (in 2019)
- http://www.backlander.ca

available from:

- Amazon.com,
- Amazon, ca,
- http://www.backlander.ca
- https://harvesthastings.ca